SWISS FONDUE

SWISS FONDUE

JENNIFER & ARNAUD FAVRE
PHOTOS BY DORIAN ROLLIN

CONTENTS

FOR MEAT EATERS

A BREATH OF FRESH AIR AND AN EXOTIC TOUCH

A LITTLE TOUR OF THE VEGETABLE GARDEN

FROM THE FRUIT TREE

Think different

A NOTE TO OUR READERS: FUN AND FANTASY WITH FONDUE

A winter evening, or après-ski, is often the occasion for a fondue. When friends and family gather around the pot, there is always an amusing tale to tell, and every get-together is sure to be unique, original and convivial. Everyone is agreed on the basic recipe. The mixture of cheeses can vary a bit, depending on the region, but the taste remains more or less the same. And that's exactly what fondue fans want, isn't it? The joy of rediscovering a familiar and satisfying taste.

Those who enjoy culinary tradition might also feel like experimenting with new tastes. And that's how it started with us. As a bit of fun — around a fondue pot, naturally. We wanted to mix savors and flavors. Our search stimulated creativity. What tastes best with cheese? What visual aspects would contribute to fresh appreciation of the supreme art of the fondue? What culinary fusions could enhance this typically Alpine art? What is a modern fondue?

Our first, slightly crazy idea was a fondue festival. This was an instant success and encouraged us to continue. Fondue ideas sprouted, and the list grew longer as interest grew in the *Compagnons du Caquelon* and their festival.

Numerous culinary specialties of the world have enjoyed waves of creativity. But not fondue. Seeing the pleasure of those who came to the festival inspired us to take our research work further and share it in this book of 52 recipes — one for every week of the year. Because a week without a fondue is a wasted week!

Jennifer and Arnaud Favre

P.S. All the recipes in this book are for four people. But don't hesitate to invite more guests. The more forks on the table, the more swords to be crossed!

SEEALPKÄSEREI

THE SWISS NATIONAL DISH

The oldest known fondue recipe appears in a cookbook by Anna Margaretha Gessner-Kitt from Zurich that dates back to 1699. Later, in the *Dictionnaire universel de cuisine pratique* (Universal Dictionary of Practical Cooking) by the Swiss Joseph Favre, published in Paris at the end of the nineteenth century, various recipes feature the word "fondue" in their titles: Italian-style soufflé fondue, Vaudois-style fondue (with Gruyère and Emmental cheese, wine and eggs), Geneva-style fondue (the same with added cream) and Piemontese fondue (Tomme or Fontina cheese, milk, butter, eggs and truffles). In the Valais-style fondue section, the author describes a bucolic meal: half a wheel of mountain cheese is held against a fire. This, of course, is raclette, which acquired its name in 1909.

At the risk of destroying the romantic myth, the fact is that fondue only conquered the culinary scene with the foundation of the *Coopérative des exportateurs suisses de fromage* (Swiss Cheese Exporters' Cooperative), which subsequently became the *Union suisse du commerce de fromage* (Swiss Cheese Marketing Board). Fondue was presented as the Swiss national dish at the New York World's Fair of 1939/1940. After the Second World War, it continued to be promoted as conducive to conviviality and part of the Swiss identity. Posters, sponsorship of the ski team, recipe books and slogans such as "FIGUGEGL" ("*Fondue isch guet und git e gueti Luune*" — Fondue tastes good and makes for a good atmosphere) ensured that the public — whether *en famille*, with friends or even in the Swiss Army — knew and thoroughly appreciated the dish. In the famous film *The Swissmakers* (1978), knowing how to make a fondue was part of the naturalization test. And that is how Switzerland became a nation of fondue lovers.

However, while the aggressive promotion of fondue as the Swiss national dish succeeded in establishing a standard, regional variations were forgotten. The experiments virtually stopped. Everyone was happy with the *moitié-moitié* variety (consisting of half Gruyère and half Vacherin Fribourgeois). Everyone? Well, no — not everyone! Read on to discover more about the original cheese mixes from Switzerland and other countries and the creative recipes that followed.

CHOOSING YOUR CHEESE

We obtain our cheese exclusively from the local dairy and encourage you to do the same, because master cheesemakers select and are thoroughly familiar with authentic basic ingredients.

The recipes in this book mostly use the best-known Swiss hard cheeses, such as Gruyère, Vacherin and Appenzell. Sheep's and goat's cheese feature as well and French cheeses such as Comté are also suitable for fondue. We recommend that you try them out and combine them to discover your own family recipe.

Would you like to create your own mix? Here are a few tips:

• Use about 200 grams of cheese per person.

• Select a mature cheese that has been ripened over a long time and the same amount of a softer, creamier cheese, according to your taste. You can mix Gruyère with Vacherin or Appenzell with Emmental for example. Use more than two kinds if you feel like it.

• Dice the soft or semi-hard cheese and coarsely grate the hard cheese. This will ensure that the different types melt at the same time when you heat them.

• Very important: add 3–4 teaspoons of potato or corn flour (US: corn starch).

A FONDUE MIX FOR EVERY REGION

FRANCE

1 - Normandy: Camembert, Pont-l'Évêque, Livarot, cream, milk, calvados, shallots

2 - Savoy: 40% Beaufort, 40% Abondance, 20% Savoy Emmental

3 - Franche-Comté: 100% Comté

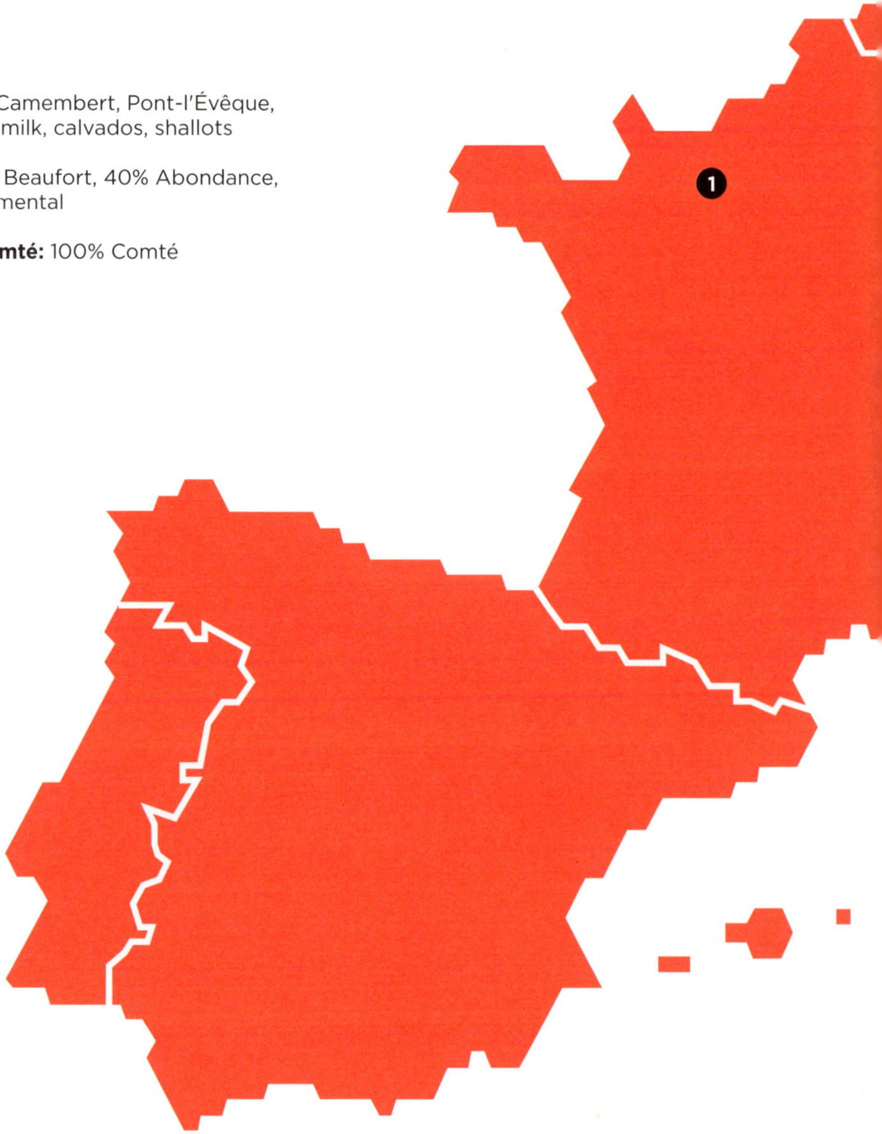

SWITZERLAND

4 - Valais: ½ Gruyère, ¼ Vacherin, ¼ Raclette AOP

5 - Neuchâtel: ½ Gruyère, ½ Emmental

6 - Fribourg: 100% Fribourg Vacherin

7 - Berne: ½ Emmental, ½ Comté

8 - Central Switzerland: ⅓ Emmental, ⅓ Gruyère, ⅓ Sbrinz

9 - Glarus: ⅔ Appenzell, ⅓ Gruyère and a little Schabziger

10 - Eastern Switzerland: ½ Appenzell, ½ Tilsit, cider instead of white wine

11 - Appenzell: ½ Appenzell, ½ Gruyère

ITALY

12/13 - Aosta Valley/Piedmont: Italian Fontina, milk, butter, eggs, white truffles

TIPS ON BREAD, POTATOES AND SIDE DISHES

Bread

With fondue, it is the taste of cheese that predominates, but to make the dish a success, it is just as important to select the right bread. The bread should not dissolve too quickly nor should it be too hard. White, semi-white and dark breads are all suitable and can be chosen according to taste. Since some people find fondue difficult to digest, we recommend avoiding wholemeal or heavier breads such as those containing nuts and/or fruit. For even more variety, check out the Swiss Bread Society's website (www.schweizerbrot.ch/www.painsuisse.ch).

It is traditional to use dry bread from the previous day. However, some people prefer fresh, crusty bread. Allow about 125 grams per person. Slice the bread, then cut the pieces into cubes, triangles, hearts or whatever shape takes your fancy.

Potatoes

Tomato fondue is traditionally accompanied by potatoes, which are also suitable for other types of fondue. They make the dish a bit lighter. Allow about 150 grams of potato per person. Peel and cook the potatoes, then cut them into pieces on your plate. Pour the cheese fondue over them or dip them into the pot. But watch out! If your piece of potato slips off the fork, you risk a penalty!

Side dishes

Pickled onions, gherkins, ground pepper, dried meat, olives, vegetables to nibble or dip into the fondue — there are no limits, just go ahead, experiment and enjoy! For anyone who likes a combination of sweet and savory, try pears, apples or pineapple pieces. If you prefer lighter dishes, serve a small mixed salad with your fondue.

WHAT TO DRINK WITH FONDUE

Wine

Tradition dictates white wine, such as a Chasselas from Vaud, a Fendant from Valais or a dry Riesling from Alsace. Some white wines from the Loire Valley are also suitable. A white Sauvignon, a Pouilly Fumé or a Muscat will go very well with a goat's or sheep's cheese fondue.

Tea

The ideal choice is a black tea, preferably drunk hot, containing bergamot oil or citrus fruit zest.

Cold drinks

There is nothing to be said against cold beverages, provided you drink slowly to avoid a lump forming in the stomach. Lager or white beer is highly refreshing as an alternative to white wine. Good, quality apple juice will also go well.

SOME SECRETS FOR A SUCCESSFUL FONDUE

Choice of pot

We strongly recommend using a cast-iron pot because it ensures better heat distribution. A fondue prepared in an earthenware pot will tend to burn more easily. A Teflon pot is the most labor saving, as it can be simply wiped clean.

How to "save" a fondue

If your cow's cheese fondue is too runny, add 1 to 2 teaspoons of potato or corn flour (US: corn starch) dissolved in 100 ml of white wine. If it is too thick, add some white wine. If your goat's or sheep's cheese fondue is too thick, add a little water. Begin with 100 ml, then add more as required. If it is too runny, dissolve 1 to 2 teaspoons of potato or corn flour (US: corn starch) in water and stir the mixture into the fondue, which should have a smooth, creamy consistency.

Cooking temperature

To prevent burning, avoid overheating your fondue, especially if you are using goat's or sheep's cheese.

Pregnancy

The risk of listeria is excluded if the cheese is heated to at least 70°C for a minimum of two minutes. A fondue melts at 80°C. Source: www.blv.admin.ch

Alcohol

Heat causes some of the alcohol to evaporate, but for a completely alcohol-free fondue substitute the wine with water, bouillon or even apple juice.

Vegan version

You can find vegetable-based alternatives on special websites such as www.vegusto.ch, which offers a ready mix, and www.theedgyveg.com, which provides an excellent recipe.

Allergies

• *Gluten:* Use gluten-free bread, potatoes or vegetables.
• *Cow's milk:* Goat's or sheep's cheese is a suitable alternative.
• *Lactose intolerance:* Hard and semi-hard cheeses are lactose-free.
Source: www.swissmilk.ch

Games

For even greater conviviality, set a challenge! Anyone who loses a piece of bread in the fondue will pay a penalty: for example, he or she must offer an aperitif at the next meeting, tell a joke or an anecdote, spell the names of those present backwards . . . There is a whole host of possible tasks.

Is the pot empty?

A crust, known as the *croustille* or *religieuse*, will form at the bottom of the pot. Scrape it out with a fork or break an egg over it. It's worth fighting for — the reward is delicious!

Digestion

Be aware that fondue is heavy on the stomach and your sleep might be disturbed if you eat late and/or drink a lot of wine with it. Here are some tips that can help digestion:

- Drink a fennel tea.
- Drink 250 ml water with a little honey and a drop of peppermint oil essence.
- Dissolve a teaspoon of bicarbonate of soda in a glass of water and drink it in one go.

Cleaning the pot

There's nothing new about this: The good old method of leaving the pot to stand overnight containing a mixture of water and washing-up liquid is the best solution. Alternatively, you can soak your pot in water containing salt or 2 teaspoons of bicarbonate of soda.

Leftovers?

Fondue is so tasty that rarely a scrap ever remains. But if by any chance there are leftovers, you can spread the cheese on a slice of bread, heat it in the oven and enjoy a most original Swiss rarebit. You can also mix the cheese into a purée or polenta or use it to cover a dish to be baked in the oven. Uncooked leftover cheese will keep for up to six months in the freezer. We advise not freezing cheese that has already been cooked.

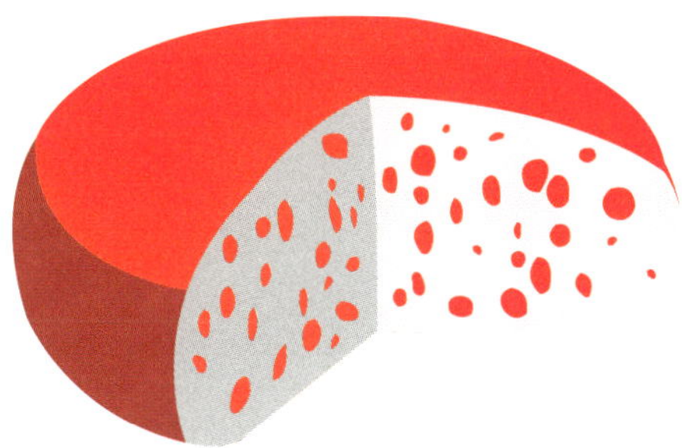

RECIPES

THE WELL-KNOWN VARIETIES

LAIT FRAIS

1 THE CLASSIC FONDUE – MADE WITH COW'S MILK CHEESE

INGREDIENTS

- 1 clove of garlic, peeled and halved
- 400 ml white wine
- 800 g fondue mix
- 500 g white bread

METHOD

1. Rub the fondue pot with the garlic, which you can remove or leave in the pot, according to taste.

2. Heat 50 ml of the wine in the pot at medium temperature.

3. Once the wine is hot, add ¼ of the fondue mix.

4. Stir throughout preparation in a figure of eight or circle with a wooden spatula, making sure that all the cheese around the edge is mixed in.

5. When the mixture begins to melt, gradually add the rest of the cheese and wine, stirring them in alternately.

6. If the fondue is too thick, add a little more wine; if it is too runny, stir in a little potato flour.

7. Once the mixture has completely melted, place the pot on a spirit or gel burner.

8. Season to taste with pepper, in the pot or on the plates.

2 FONDUE WITH FRESH BOLETUS MUSHROOMS – FLAVORS OF THE FOREST

INGREDIENTS

- 1 clove of garlic, peeled and halved
- 400 ml white wine
- 800 g fondue mix
- 200 g fresh boletus mushrooms, finely chopped (if using dried mushrooms, soak them for 30 minutes in lukewarm water)
- 500 g white bread

METHOD

1. Rub the fondue pot with the garlic, which you can then leave in the pot or remove, according to taste.

2. Heat about 50 ml of the wine in the pot at medium temperature.

3. As soon as the wine starts to heat, add about ¼ of your fondue mix.

4. Stir throughout preparation in a figure of eight or circle with a wooden spatula, making sure that all the cheese around the edge is mixed in.

5. When the mixture begins to melt, gradually add more of the cheese and wine, stirring them in alternately.

6. Add the mushrooms when you have mixed in about half the cheese.

7. Once the mixture has completely melted, place the pot on a spirit or gel burner.

8. Season to taste with pepper, in the pot or on the plates.

3 PIQUANT FONDUE WITH GREEN PEPPER

INGREDIENTS

- 1 clove of garlic, peeled and halved
- 400 ml white wine
- 800 g fondue mix
- 8 teaspoons green pepper
- 500 g white bread

METHOD

1. Rub the bottom of your fondue pot with the garlic, which you can then leave in the pot or remove, according to taste.

2. Heat about 50 ml of the wine in the pot at medium temperature.

3. As soon as the wine is hot, add about ¼ of your fondue mix, stirring round the edge toward the center throughout preparation.

4. When the cheese begins to melt, gradually stir in the rest alternately with the wine, and add about half of the pepper.

5. Taste and add more pepper if required.

6. Once the mixture has completely melted, place the pot on a spirit or gel burner.

4 FRUITY FONDUE WITH APPLE SCHNAPPS

INGREDIENTS

- 1 clove of garlic, peeled and halved
- 300 ml white wine
- 800 g fondue mix
- 60 to 80 ml apple schnapps (for example Morand)
- 500 g white bread

METHOD

1. Start by rubbing the fondue pot with the garlic, which you can then leave in the pot or remove, according to taste.

2. Heat about 50 ml of the wine in the pot at medium temperature.

3. As soon as the wine is hot, add about ¼ of your fondue mix.

4. Stir throughout preparation in a zigzag or circle with a wooden spatula, making sure that all the cheese around the edge is mixed in.

5. When the cheese begins to melt, gradually stir in the rest alternately with wine. Once you have worked in ¾ of the fondue mix, add half the apple schnapps and continue to stir a little.

6. Taste and add more apple schnapps if required.

7. Once the mixture has completely melted, place the pot on a spirit or gel burner.

8. Season to taste with pepper, in the pot or on the plates.

S

AROMATIC FONDUE WITH WHOLE-GRAIN MUSTARD

INGREDIENTS

- 1 clove of garlic, peeled and halved
- 400 ml white wine
- 800 g fondue mix
- 6 to 8 teaspoons whole-grain mustard
- 500 g white bread

TIP

Add a little espelette (chili) pepper for variety.

METHOD

1. Rub the fondue pot with the garlic, which you can then leave in the pot or remove, according to taste.

2. Heat about 50 ml of the wine in the pot at medium temperature.

3. Once the wine is hot, add ¼ of your fondue mix and let it melt, stirring throughout preparation.

4. Gradually stir in more wine and cheese. When ¾ of the cheese has melted, add half of the mustard.

5. Taste, and add the rest of the mustard or more if required.

6. Once the mixture has completely melted, place the pot on a spirit or gel burner.

7. Season to taste with pepper, in the pot or on the plates.

FESTIVE VARIATIONS

6 THE VALAIS TOUCH – WITH APRICOT SCHNAPPS

INGREDIENTS

- 1 clove of garlic, peeled and halved
- 300 ml white wine
- 800 g fondue mix
- 60 to 80 ml apricot schnapps (Morand abricotine, for example)
- 500 g white bread

TIP

For an even fruitier fondue, add small pieces of dried apricot.

METHOD

1. Rub the fondue pot with the garlic, which you can then leave in the pot or remove, according to taste.

2. Heat about 50 ml of the wine in the pot at medium temperature.

3. When the wine is hot, add about ¼ of your fondue mix.

4. Stir in a zigzag with a wooden spatula, making sure that all the cheese around the edge is mixed in.

5. When the mixture begins to melt, gradually add the rest of the cheese and wine, stirring them in alternately. When you have worked in ¾ of the fondue mix, pour in half of the apricot schnapps and stir gently. Important! Taste first and add more schnapps if required.

6. Once the mixture has completely melted, place the pot on a spirit or gel burner.

7. Season to taste with pepper, in the pot or on the plates.

7 FONDUE WITH BEER – LIGHT AS BUBBLES

INGREDIENTS

- 1 clove of garlic, peeled and halved
- 400 ml strong, hoppy beer (Lupulus Blonde, for example)
- 800 g fondue mix
- 500 g white bread

TIP

You can use any lager, dark or red beer — the taste will vary accordingly. Dark beer, for example, gives an attractive color and a caramel after-taste. Lager makes the fondue lighter without masking the taste of the cheese.

METHOD

1. Rub the fondue pot with the garlic, which you can then leave in the pot or remove, according to taste.

2. Heat about 50 ml of the beer in the pot at medium temperature.

3. When the beer starts to heat up, add about ¼ of your fondue mix.

4. Stir thoroughly, making sure that all the cheese around the edge is mixed in.

5. When the mixture begins to melt, gradually add the rest of the cheese and beer, stirring them in alternately.

6. If the fondue is too thick, add a little more beer; if it is too runny, add some potato flour.

7. Once the mixture has completely melted, place the pot on a spirit or gel burner.

8. Season to taste with pepper, in the pot or on the plates.

8 AMBER FONDUE – GILDED WITH CALVADOS

INGREDIENTS

- 1 clove of garlic, peeled and halved
- 300 ml white wine
- 800 g fondue mix
- 60 to 80 ml calvados
- 500 g white bread

METHOD

1. Rub the fondue pot with the garlic, which you can then leave in the pot or remove, according to taste.

2. Heat about 50 ml of the wine in the pot at medium temperature.

3. When the wine begins to heat up, add ¼ of your fondue mix.

4. Stir in a figure of eight or circle, making sure that all the cheese around the edge is mixed in.

5. Once the mixture begins to melt, gradually add the rest of the wine and cheese, stirring them in alternately. When you have worked in ¾ of the fondue mix, pour in half the calvados and stir gently. Taste before adding the rest of the calvados and stir in more if required.

6. When the mixture has completely melted, place the pot on a spirit or gel burner.

7. Season to taste with pepper, in the pot or on the plates.

9 FIZZY FONDUE WITH CHAMPAGNE

INGREDIENTS

- 1 clove of garlic, peeled and halved
- 400 ml brut Champagne
- 800 g fondue mix
- 500 g white bread

METHOD

1. Rub the fondue pot with the garlic, which you can then leave in the pot or remove, according to taste.

2. Heat about 50 ml of the champagne in the pot at medium temperature.

3. When the Champagne begins to heat up, add ¼ of your fondue mix.

4. Stir thoroughly, making sure that all the cheese around the edge is mixed in.

5. When mixture begins to melt, gradually add the rest of the cheese and champagne, stirring them in alternately.

6. If the fondue is too thick, add a little more Champagne; if it is too thin, stir in some potato flour.

7. Once the mixture has completely melted, place the pot on a spirit or gel burner.

8. Season to taste with pepper, in the pot or on the plates.

10 FONDUE WITH CIDER – AMAZINGLY LIGHT AND TANGY

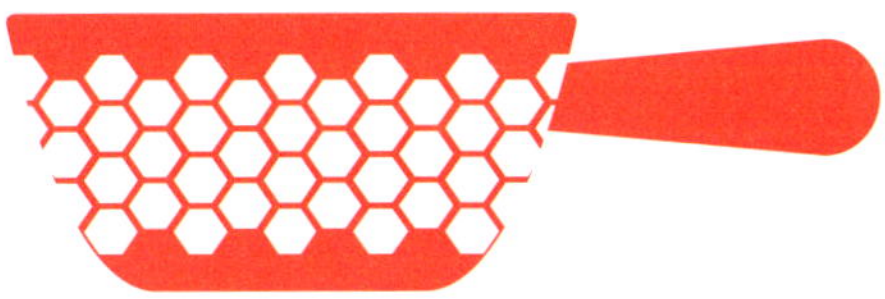

INGREDIENTS

- 1 clove of garlic, peeled and halved
- 400 ml cider, with or without alcohol
- 800 g fondue mix
- 500 g white bread

METHOD

1. First of all, rub the fondue pot with the garlic, which you can then leave in the pot or remove, according to taste.

2. Heat about 50 ml of the cider in the pot at medium temperature.

3. When the cider is hot, add ¼ of your fondue mix.

4. Stir thoroughly, making sure that all the cheese around the edge is mixed in.

5. When the mixture begins to melt, gradually add the rest of the cheese, stirring it in alternately with the cider.

6. If the fondue is too thick, add a little more cider; if it is too runny, stir in some potato flour.

7. Once the mixture has completely melted, place the pot on a spirit or gel burner.

8. Season to taste with pepper, in the pot or on the plates.

11 FONDUE WITH COGNAC – A SUCCESS IN ALL SEASONS

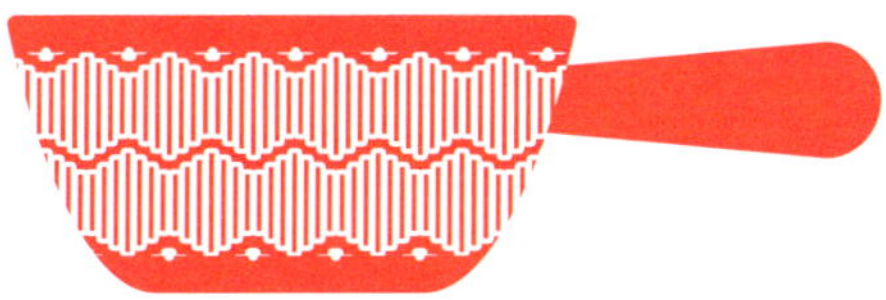

INGREDIENTS

- 1 clove of garlic, peeled and halved
- 300 ml white wine
- 800 g fondue mix
- 60 to 80 ml cognac
- 500 g white bread

METHOD

1. Rub the fondue pot with the garlic, which you can then leave in the pot or remove, according to taste.

2. Heat 50 ml of the wine in the pot at medium temperature.

3. When the wine is hot, add ¼ of your fondue mix.

4. Stir thoroughly in a figure of eight or circle, making sure that all the cheese around the edge is mixed in.

5. When the mixture begins to melt, gradually add the rest of the cheese and wine, stirring them in alternately, then pour in half the cognac.

6. Taste and add more cognac if required.

7. Once the mixture has completely melted, place the pot on a spirit or gel burner.

8. Season to taste with pepper, in the pot or on the plates.

12 FUSION FONDUE – WITH BELL PEPPERS AND GRAPPA

INGREDIENTS

- 1 clove of garlic, peeled and halved
- 300 ml white wine
- 800 g fondue mix
- ¾ of a red or orange bell pepper, diced
- 40 to 60 ml grappa
- 500 g white bread

TIP

For those who can't digest bell pepper, remove the skin. Wash the pepper, put it in the oven, which you have set to grill, and leave it for 15 to 20 minutes, turning it every five minutes. This will make it easy to peel.

METHOD

1. Rub the fondue pot with the garlic, which you can then leave in the pot or remove, according to taste.

2. Heat 50 ml of the wine in the pot at medium temperature.

3. When the wine begins to heat up, add the diced bell pepper and simmer for about a minute.

4. Once the wine is hot, add ¼ of your fondue mix.

5. Stir thoroughly in a zigzag or circle, making sure that all the cheese around the edge and the bell pepper are thoroughly mixed in.

6. When the mixture begins to melt, gradually add the rest of the cheese and wine and half of the grappa.

7. Taste and add more grappa if required.

8. Once the mixture has completely melted, place the pot on a spirit or gel burner.

9. Season to taste with pepper, in the pot or on the plates.

13 FONDUE LACED WITH PORT

INGREDIENTS

- 1 clove of garlic, peeled and halved
- 300 ml white wine
- 800 g fondue mix
- 60 to 80 ml red or white port
- 500 g white bread

METHOD

1. Rub the fondue pot with the garlic, which you can then leave in the pot or remove, according to taste.

2. Heat 50 ml of the wine in the pot at medium temperature.

3. When the wine is hot, add ¼ of your fondue mix.

4. Stir in a figure of eight or circle, making sure that all the cheese around the edge is mixed in.

5. When the mixture begins to melt, gradually add the rest of the cheese and wine and half of the port.

6. Taste and add more port if required.

7. Once the mixture has completely melted, place the pot on a spirit or gel burner.

8. Season to taste with pepper, in the pot or on the plates.

14 FONDUE *EXQUISITE* WITH RED WINE

INGREDIENTS

- 1 clove of garlic, peeled and halved
- 400 ml red wine, Humagne for example
- 800 g fondue mix
- 500 g white bread

TIP

Serve the same red wine you have used to make the fondue or, for a lighter meal, a white wine.

METHOD

1. Rub the fondue pot with the garlic, which you can then leave in the pot or remove, according to taste.

2. Heat about 50 ml of the red wine in the pot at medium temperature.

3. When the wine is hot, add ¼ of your fondue mix.

4. Stir in a figure of eight or circle, making sure that all the cheese around the edge is mixed in.

5. When the mixture begins to melt, gradually add the rest of the cheese, stirring it in alternately with the red wine.

6. Once the mixture has completely melted, place the pot on a spirit or gel burner.

7. Season to taste with pepper, in the pot or on the plates.

15 FONDUE WITH WHISK(E)Y – A CARAMEL TOUCH

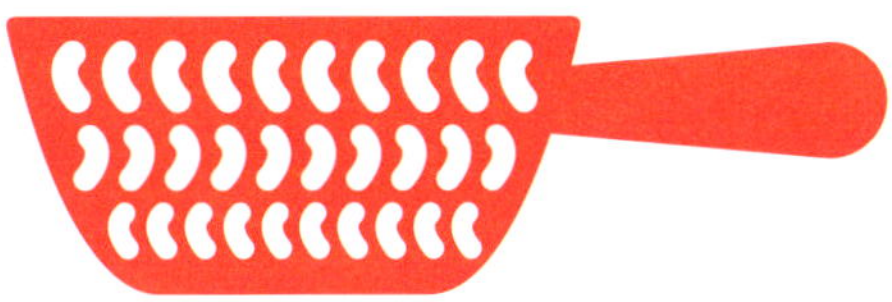

INGREDIENTS

- 1 clove of garlic, peeled and halved
- 300 ml white wine
- 800 g fondue mix
- 40 to 60 ml Scotch or Irish whisk(e)y
- 500 g white bread

METHOD

1. Rub the fondue pot with the garlic, which you can then leave in the pot or remove, according to taste.

2. Heat 50 ml of the wine in the pot at medium temperature.

3. When the wine heats up, add ¼ of your fondue mix.

4. Stir thoroughly with a spatula, making sure that all the cheese around the edge is mixed in.

5. When the mixture begins to melt, gradually add more wine and cheese, stirring them in alternately.

6. Once you have worked in ¾ of the fondue mix, stir in 40 ml whisk(e)y to start with. Taste before adding the rest and stir in more if required.

7. When the mixture has completely melted, place the pot on a spirit or gel burner.

8. Season to taste with pepper, in the pot or on the plates.

16 FONDUE WITH WILLIAMS PEAR SCHNAPPS

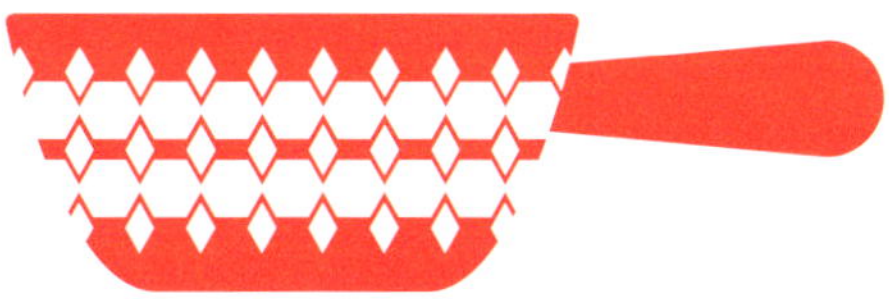

INGREDIENTS

- 1 clove of garlic, peeled and halved
- 300 ml white wine
- 800 g fondue mix
- 60 to 80 ml Williams pear schnapps, for example Williamine®
- 2 pears, peeled and cut into small pieces
- 500 g white bread

METHOD

1. Rub the fondue pot with the garlic, which you can then leave in the pot or remove, according to taste.

2. Heat 50 ml of the wine in the pot at medium temperature.

3. When the wine is hot, add ¼ of your fondue mix.

4. Stir thoroughly in a figure of eight or circle, making sure that all the cheese around the edge is mixed in.

5. When the mixture begins to melt, gradually add the rest of the cheese and wine, the pears and some of the schnapps, stirring them in alternately.

6. Taste and add more schnapps if required.

7. Once the mixture has completely melted, place the pot on a spirit or gel burner.

8. Season to taste with pepper, in the pot or on the plates. You're ready to taste your vitamin-rich dish!

GOAT´S AND SHEEP´S CHEESE

17 NO-FRILLS FONDUE WITH GOAT'S CHEESE

INGREDIENTS

- 1 clove of garlic, peeled and halved
- 400 ml white wine
- 800 g goat's cheese fondue mix
- 500 g white bread

IMPORTANT

Avoid overheating the fondue — goat's cheese is delicate and needs to be heated gently.

METHOD

1. Rub the fondue pot with the garlic, which you can then leave in the pot or remove, according to taste.

2. Very gently heat 50 ml of the wine in the pot at medium temperature.

3. When the wine is hot, add ¼ of your fondue mix.

4. Stir gently in a figure of eight or circle, making sure that all the cheese around the edge is mixed in.

5. When the mixture begins to melt, gradually add the rest of the cheese and wine, stirring them in alternately.

6. Once the mixture has completely melted, place the pot on a spirit or gel burner.

7. Season to taste with pepper, in the pot or on the plates.

18 A FONDUE MIRACLE – GOAT'S CHEESE, HONEY AND WALNUTS

INGREDIENTS

- 1 clove of garlic, peeled and halved
- 400 ml white wine
- 800 g goat's cheese fondue mix
- 6 to 8 teaspoons liquid honey
- A handful of finely chopped walnuts
- 500 g white bread

IMPORTANT

Avoid overheating the fondue — goat's cheese is delicate and needs to be heated gently.

TIP

Mountain honey is floral, transparent and solid. For this recipe, we recommend forest honey, which is more highly flavored, darker and runnier.

METHOD

1. Rub the fondue pot with the garlic, which you can then leave in the pot or remove, according to taste.

2. Heat 50 ml of the wine in the pot at medium temperature.

3. When the wine starts to heat up, add the walnuts and simmer for about a minute.

4. Add another 50 ml wine.

5. Once the wine is hot, add ¼ of the fondue mix.

6. Stir gently in a figure of eight or circle, making sure that all the cheese around the edge is mixed in.

7. Once the mixture begins to melt, gradually add the rest of the cheese and wine, stirring them in alternately. When you have worked in ¾ of the fondue mix, add half of the honey and continue to stir gently.

8. Taste the mixture and add more honey to taste.

9. When the mixture has completely melted, place the pot on a spirit or gel burner.

10. Season to taste with pepper, in the pot or on the plates.

19 QUEBEC-STYLE FONDUE WITH GOAT'S CHEESE AND MAPLE SYRUP

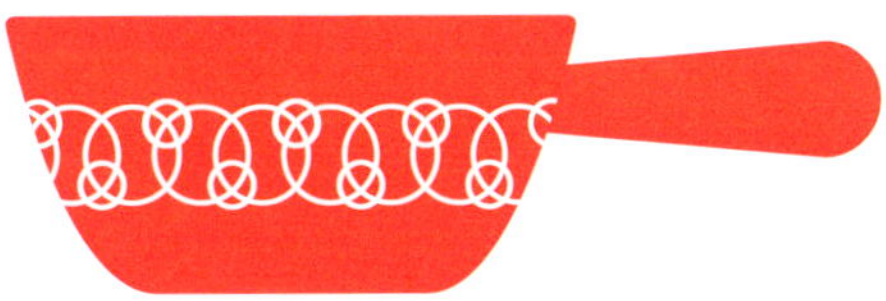

INGREDIENTS

- 1 clove of garlic, peeled and halved
- 400 ml white wine
- 800 g goat's cheese fondue mix
- 6 to 8 teaspoons maple syrup
- 500 g white bread

IMPORTANT

Avoid overheating the fondue — goat's cheese is delicate and needs to be heated gently.

TIP

Maple syrup mellows the taste of the cheese, making this fondue ideal for anyone who's skeptical about goat's cheese!

METHOD

1. Rub the fondue pot with the garlic, which you can then leave in the pot or remove, according to taste.

2. Gently heat 50 ml of the wine in the pot at medium temperature.

3. Once the wine is hot, add ¼ of the fondue mix.

4. Stir gently in a figure of eight or circle, making sure that all the cheese around the edge is mixed in.

5. As soon as the mixture begins to melt, gradually add the rest of the wine and cheese, stirring them in alternately. When you have worked in ¾ of the fondue mix, add half of the maple syrup and stir again gently.

6. Taste the mixture and add more maple syrup as required.

7. Once the mixture has completely melted, place the pot on a spirit or gel burner.

8. Season to taste with pepper, in the pot or on the plates.

20 NO-FRILLS FONDUE WITH SHEEP'S CHEESE

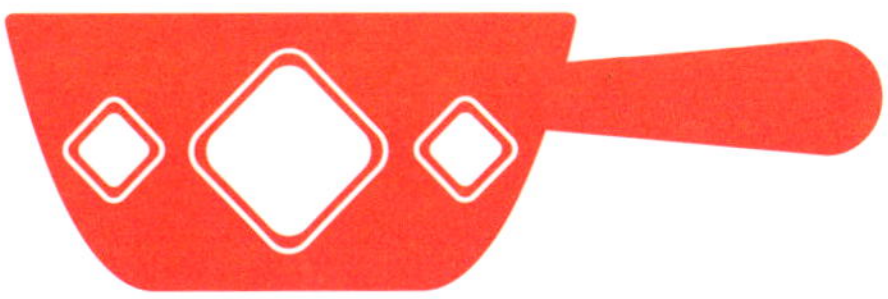

INGREDIENTS

- 1 clove of garlic, peeled and halved
- 400 ml white wine
- 800 g sheep's cheese fondue mix
- 500 g white bread

IMPORTANT

Avoid overheating the fondue — sheep's cheese is delicate and needs to be heated gently.

METHOD

1. Rub the fondue pot with the garlic, which you can then leave in the pot or remove, according to taste.

2. Gently heat 50 ml of the wine in the pot at medium temperature.

3. Once the wine is hot, add ¼ of the fondue mix.

4. Stir gently in a figure of eight or circle, making sure that all the cheese around the edge is mixed in.

5. When the mixture begins to melt, gradually add the rest of the cheese and wine, stirring them in alternately.

6. When the mixture has completely melted, place the pot on a spirit or gel burner.

7. Season to taste with pepper, in the pot or on the plates.

21 EXOTIC SHEEP'S CHEESE FONDUE WITH CURRY AND PINEAPPLE

INGREDIENTS

- 1 clove of garlic, peeled and halved
- 400 ml white wine
- 800 g sheep's cheese fondue mix
- 6 to 8 teaspoons curry powder, according to taste
- 200 g fresh pineapple, diced
- 500 g white bread

IMPORTANT

Avoid overheating the fondue — sheep's cheese is delicate and needs to be heated gently.

METHOD

1. Rub the fondue pot with the garlic, which you can then leave in the pot or remove, according to taste.

2. Gently heat about 50 ml of the wine in the pot at medium temperature.

3. When the wine starts to heat up, add the pineapple and simmer for one minute.

4. Add about ¼ of the fondue mix.

5. Stir very gently in a figure of eight or circle, making sure that all the cheese around the edge is mixed in.

6. When the cheese begins to melt, gradually add the rest alternately with the wine and some of the curry powder. Take your time.

7. Taste the mixture and add more curry if required.

8. Once the mixture has completely melted, place the pot on a spirit or gel burner.

9. Season to taste with pepper, in the pot or on the plates.

22 A HARMONIOUS FONDUE DUET OF SHEEP'S CHEESE AND TOMATOES

INGREDIENTS

- 1 clove of garlic, peeled and halved
- 300 ml white wine
- 800 g sheep's cheese fondue mix
- 250 g homemade tomato sauce (see page 83)
- 500 g white bread or 600 g potatoes in their skins

IMPORTANT

Avoid overheating the fondue — sheep's cheese is delicate and needs to be heated gently.

TIP

Tomato fondue is traditionally eaten with potatoes rather than bread.

METHOD

1. Rub the fondue pot with the garlic, which you can then leave in the pot or remove, according to taste.

2. Gently heat about 50 ml of the wine in the pot at medium temperature.

3. Once the wine is hot, add ¼ of the fondue mix.

4. Stir gently in a figure of eight or circle, making sure that all the cheese around the edge is mixed in.

5. When the mixture begins to melt, gradually add the rest of the cheese and wine, stirring them in alternately. When you have worked in ¾ of the fondue mix, add the tomato sauce.

6. Once the mixture has completely melted, place the pot on a spirit or gel burner.

7. Season to taste with pepper, in the pot or on the plates.

TOMATO SAUCE

INGREDIENTS

- ½ a sugar lump
- 4 to 5 basil leaves
- 1 clove of garlic
- 1 tablespoon olive oil
- 1 medium-sized yellow onion, finely chopped
- 4 large, ripe tomatoes
- Salt, pepper

METHOD

1. Boil a large quantity of water. Cut a cross in the bottom of the tomatoes to facilitate peeling and immerse them in the water for one minute.

2. Peel the tomatoes, then heat the olive oil in a small pan. Add the chopped onion and fry gently until transparent.

3. Cut the tomatoes into large pieces and add them on top of the garlic. Stir in the sugar, salt and pepper, then cook the mixture at low temperature, allowing a good 15 minutes.

4. Once the tomatoes have softened, use a liquidizer or masher to produce a smooth purée. Simmer for five minutes, then add the basil. Your sauce is ready!

FOR MEAT EATERS

23 FONDUE WITH CERVELAS SAUSAGE

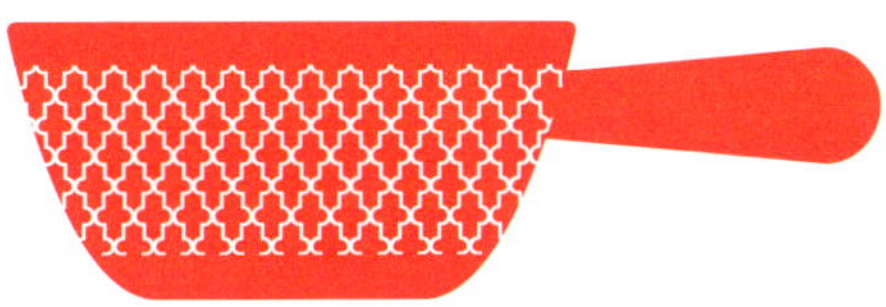

INGREDIENTS

- 1 clove of garlic, peeled and halved
- 400 ml white wine
- 800 g fondue mix
- 1 cervelas* sausage, finely diced
- 500 g white bread

* If you cannot obtain a cervelas, you can use another, similar type of sausage such as a frankfurter or a saveloy.

METHOD

1. Begin by rubbing the fondue pot with the garlic, which you can then leave in the pot or remove, according to taste.

2. Gently heat about 50 ml of the wine in the pot at medium temperature.

3. When the wine starts to heat up, add the finely diced cervelas and simmer for about a minute.

4. Add another 50 ml wine and heat gently.

5. Once the wine is hot, add ¼ of the fondue mix.

6. Stir in a figure of eight or circle, making sure that all the cheese around the edge is mixed in.

7. When the mixture begins to melt, add the rest of the wine and cheese, stirring them in alternately.

8. When the mixture has completely melted, place the pot on a spirit or gel burner.

9. Season to taste with pepper, in the pot or on the plates.

24 CRISPY FONDUE WITH A CRUMBLE OF DRIED MEAT

INGREDIENTS

- 1 clove of garlic, peeled and halved
- 400 ml white wine
- 800 g fondue mix
- Dried meat crumble (see page 91)
- 500 g white bread

METHOD

1. Begin by rubbing the fondue pot with the garlic, which you can then leave in the pot or remove, according to taste.

2. Gently heat about 50 ml of the wine in the pot at medium temperature.

3. Once the wine is hot, add ¼ of the fondue mix.

4. Stir in a figure of eight or circle, making sure that all the cheese around the edge is mixed in.

5. When the mixture begins to melt, gradually add the rest of the cheese and wine, stirring them in alternately.

6. Once the fondue is ready, sprinkle the crumble on top.

7. Place the pot on a spirit or gel burner.

8. Season to taste with pepper, in the pot or on the plates.

DRIED MEAT CRUMBLE

INGREDIENTS

- 2 cloves of garlic
- 2 shallots
- 200 g dried meat

METHOD

1. Finely chop the garlic and shallots.

2. Sauté the garlic, shallots and dried meat in a non-stick pan.

NOGENT
INOX classic FRANCE

25 SPICY FONDUE WITH CHORIZO

INGREDIENTS

- 1 clove of garlic, peeled and halved
- 400 ml white wine
- 800 g fondue mix
- 200 g chorizo, finely chopped
- 500 g white bread

METHOD

1. Rub the fondue pot with the garlic, which you can then leave in the pot or remove, according to taste.

2. Gently heat about 50 ml of the wine in the pot at medium temperature.

3. When the wine begins to heat up, add the chopped chorizo and simmer for about a minute.

4. Add ¼ of the fondue mix and a little more of the wine.

5. Stir in a zigzag or circle, making sure that all the cheese around the edge is mixed in.

6. When the mixture begins to melt, gradually add the rest of the cheese and wine, stirring them in alternately.

7. Once the mixture has completely melted, place the pot on a spirit or gel burner.

8. Season to taste with pepper, in the pot or on the plates.

26 THE INDISPENSABLE FONDUE – WITH UNCOOKED HAM

INGREDIENTS

• 1 clove of garlic, peeled and halved

• 400 ml white wine

• 800 g fondue mix

• 150 g uncooked ham, finely chopped

• 500 g white bread

METHOD

1. Rub the fondue pot with the garlic, which you can then leave in the pot or remove, according to taste.

2. Gently heat 50 ml of the wine in the pot at medium temperature.

3. Once the wine is hot, add ¼ of the fondue mix.

4. Stir thoroughly to make sure that all the cheese around the edge is mixed in and to prevent it from sticking to the bottom of the pot.

5. When the cheese begins to melt, stir in the rest bit by bit alternately with the wine, then add the uncooked ham.

6. When the mixture has completely melted, place the pot on a spirit or gel burner and get ready to enjoy this tasty fondue.

7. Season to taste with pepper, in the pot or on the plates.

27 THE MUST-HAVE FONDUE WITH HAM AND MADEIRA

INGREDIENTS

- 1 clove of garlic, peeled and halved
- 300 ml white wine
- 800 g fondue mix
- 200 g cooked ham, cut into small cubes
- 2 tablespoons tomato purée
- 40 ml Madeira
- 1 tablespoon Italian mixed herbs
- 500 g white bread

METHOD

1. Rub the fondue pot with the garlic, which you can then leave in the pot or remove, according to taste.

2. Heat 50 ml of the wine in the pot at medium temperature.

3. When the wine begins to heat up, add the ham and simmer for about a minute.

4. Add ¼ of the fondue mix, then a little of the white wine.

5. Stir, making sure that all the cheese around the edge is mixed in.

6. When the mixture begins to melt, gradually add the rest of the cheese alternately with the wine, then stir in the tomato purée, half the Madeira and the herbs.

7. Taste and add more Madeira as required.

8. Once the mixture has completely melted, place the pot on a spirit or gel burner.

9. Season to taste with pepper, in the pot or on the plates.

28 THE REAL THING – FONDUE WITH BACON PIECES AND ONION

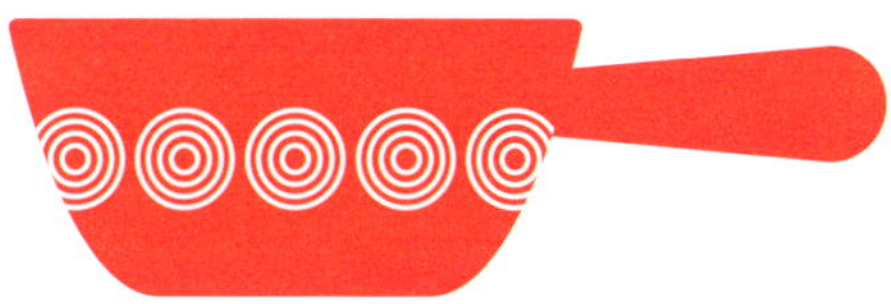

INGREDIENTS

- 1 clove of garlic, peeled and halved
- 400 ml white wine
- 800 g fondue mix
- 125 g bacon pieces
- 1 medium-sized onion, finely chopped
- 500 g white bread

NOTE

This is the specialty of the *Compagnons du Caquelon*!

TIP

The bacon might make the fondue too thick. If so, add a little more wine. If the fondue is too runny, add a little potato flour.

METHOD

1. Fry the bacon pieces and chop the onion.

2. Rub the fondue pot with the garlic, which you can then leave in the pot or remove, according to taste.

3. Heat 50 ml of the wine in the fondue pot at medium temperature.

4. When the wine begins to heat up, add the bacon pieces and chopped onion and simmer for about a minute.

5. Add ¼ of the fondue mix and a little more of the white wine.

6. Stir in a figure of eight or circle, making sure that all the cheese around the edge is mixed in.

7. When the mixture begins to melt, gradually add the rest of the cheese and wine, stirring them in alternately.

8. Once the mixture has completely melted, place the pot on a spirit or gel burner.

9. Season to taste with pepper, in the pot or on the plates.

29 OUTDOOR SUMMER FONDUE WITH MERGUEZ SAUSAGES

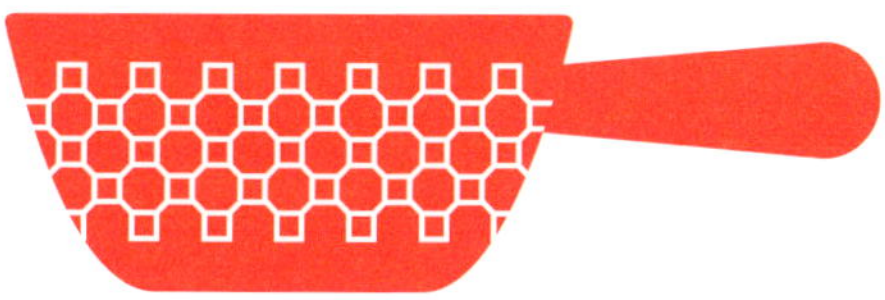

INGREDIENTS

- 1 clove of garlic, peeled and halved
- 400 ml white wine
- 800 g fondue mix
- 150 g merguez sausages
- 500 g white bread

METHOD

1. Cut the merguez into small pieces and fry them.

2. Rub the fondue pot with the garlic, which you can then leave in the pot or remove, according to taste.

3. Heat 50 ml of the wine in the pot at medium temperature.

4. When the wine begins to heat up, add the merguez and simmer for about a minute.

5. Add ¼ of the fondue mix and a little more of the white wine.

6. Stir in a figure of eight or circle, making sure that all the cheese around the edge is mixed in.

7. When the mixture begins to melt, gradually add the rest of the cheese and wine, stirring them in alternately. Savor the intoxicating aroma of the merguez as they bind with the cheese!

8. Once the mixture has completely melted, place the pot on a spirit or gel burner.

9. Season to taste with pepper, in the pot or on the plates.

A BREATH OF FRESH AIR AND AN EXOTIC TOUCH

30 FONDUE PEPPED UP WITH PAPRIKA

INGREDIENTS

• 1 clove of garlic, peeled and halved

• 400 ml white wine

• 800 g fondue mix

• 6 to 8 teaspoons paprika powder, according to taste

• 500 g white bread

METHOD

1. Rub the fondue pot with the garlic, which you can then leave in the pot or remove, according to taste.

2. Heat 50 ml of the wine in the fondue pot at medium temperature.

3. Once the wine is hot, add ¼ of the fondue mix.

4. Stir in a figure of eight or circle, making sure that all the cheese around the edge is mixed in.

5. When the mixture begins to melt, gradually add the rest of the cheese and wine and half the paprika.

6. Taste and add more paprika if required.

7. Once the mixture has completely melted, place the pot on a spirit or gel burner.

8. Season to taste with pepper, in the pot or on the plates.

31 FIERY FONDUE SEASONED WITH CHILI

INGREDIENTS

- 1 clove of garlic, peeled and halved
- 400 ml white wine
- 800 g fondue mix
- 8 teaspoons chili powder or 1 small red chili, finely chopped
- 500 g white bread

METHOD

1. Rub the fondue pot with the garlic, which you can then leave in the pot or remove, according to taste.

2. Heat 50 ml of the wine in the fondue pot at medium temperature, add the chili pieces and simmer. (If you are using chili powder, see instructions under step 5).

3. Add ¼ of the fondue mix and stir in a figure of eight or circle, making sure that all the cheese around the edge is mixed in.

4. When the mixture begins to melt, gradually add the rest of the cheese and wine, stirring them in alternately. Work in half of the chili powder to begin with, then mix thoroughly.

5. Taste and add the rest of the chili powder, add more if required.

6. Once the fondue is ready, place the pot on a spirit or gel burner.

7. Season to taste with pepper, in the pot or on the plates.

32 FONDUE WITH GINGER AND LEMON – FRESH AND TANGY

INGREDIENTS

- 1 clove of garlic, peeled and halved
- 400 ml white wine
- 800 g fondue mix
- 50 g ginger
- 60 to 80 ml fresh lemon juice
- 500 g white bread

METHOD

1. Begin by rubbing the fondue pot with the garlic, which you can then leave in the pot or remove, according to taste.

2. Heat 50 ml of the wine in the fondue pot at medium temperature.

3. Peel the ginger and dice it finely.

4. When the wine begins to heat up, simmer the ginger for about a minute, stirring gently with a wooden spatula.

5. Add ¼ of the fondue mix.

6. Stir, making sure that all the cheese around the edge is mixed in.

7. When the mixture begins to melt, gradually stir in the rest of the cheese alternately with the wine, then add half of the lemon juice.

8. Taste and add the rest of the lemon juice, or more if required.

9. Once the fondue is ready, place the pot on a spirit or gel burner. You are ready to give your taste buds a treat!

10. Season to taste with pepper, in the pot or on the plates.

33 FONDUE WITH MOROCCAN CUMIN

INGREDIENTS

- 1 clove of garlic, peeled and halved
- 400 ml white wine
- 800 g fondue mix
- 4 to 5 teaspoons cumin seeds
- 500 g white bread

METHOD

1. Rub the fondue pot with the garlic, which you can then leave in the pot or remove, according to taste.

2. Heat 50 ml of the wine in the fondue pot at medium temperature.

3. When the wine is hot, add about ¼ of the fondue mix.

4. Stir throughout preparation, making sure that all the cheese at the edge is mixed in.

5. When the mixture begins to melt, gradually stir in the rest of the cheese alternately with the wine. Once you have worked in ¾ of the mixture, add half the cumin and continue to stir a little.

6. Taste and add the rest of the cumin, add a little more if required.

7. Once the mixture has completely melted, place the pot on a spirit or gel burner.

8. Season to taste with pepper, in the pot or on the plates.

34 FONDUE SPICED WITH MILD CURRY

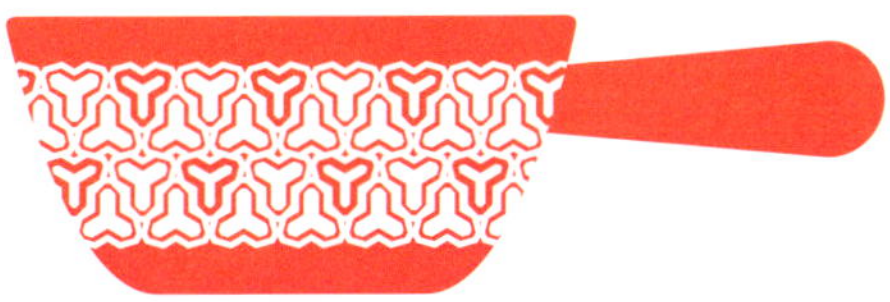

INGREDIENTS

- 1 clove of garlic, peeled and halved
- 400 ml white wine
- 800 g fondue mix
- 6 to 8 teaspoons mild curry powder, according to taste
- 500 g white bread

TIP

To vary the taste, replace the mild curry with Madras curry, garam masala, or red or yellow Thai curry paste.

METHOD

1. Rub the fondue pot with the garlic, which you can then leave in the pot or remove, according to taste.

2. Heat 50 ml of the wine in the fondue pot at medium temperature.

3. When the wine is hot, add ¼ of the fondue mix.

4. Stir in a figure of eight or circle, making sure that all the cheese around the edge is mixed in.

5. When the mixture begins to melt, gradually add the rest of the cheese and wine, and half the curry powder. See how your fondue takes on a beautiful golden shade!

6. Taste and add the rest of the curry powder, add a little more if required.

7. Once the mixture has completely melted, place the pot on a spirit or gel burner.

8. Season to taste with pepper, in the pot or on the plates.

35 MEXICAN-STYLE FONDUE – A RAY OF SUNSHINE

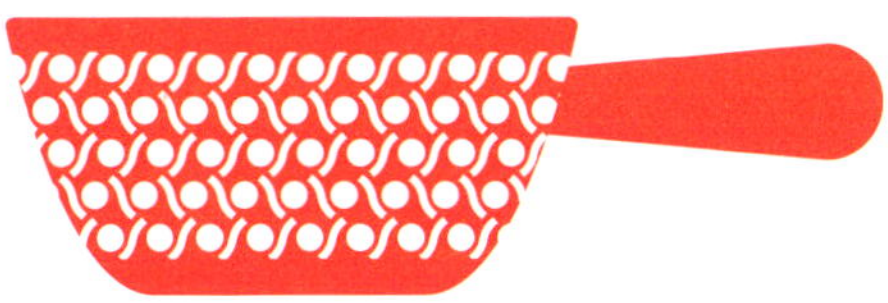

INGREDIENTS

- 1 clove of garlic, peeled and halved
- 400 ml white wine
- 800 g fondue mix
- 50 g fresh sweetcorn
- 50 g red kidney beans
- 50 g red bell pepper
- 50 g cooked minced beef
- 3 teaspoons chili powder
- 40 ml Tequila
- 500 g white bread

TIP

Have extra fun with this fondue by adding nachos! Stir a little more white wine into the mix to make sure the fondue is liquid enough and the nachos don't break.

METHOD

1. Rub the fondue pot with the garlic, which you can then leave in the pot or remove, according to taste.

2. Heat 50 ml of the wine in the fondue pot at medium temperature.

3. When the wine begins to heat up, add all the ingredients and simmer for about a minute.

4. Add another 50 ml wine, followed by ¼ of the fondue mix. Enjoy the aroma!

5. Stir in a figure of eight or circle, making sure that all the cheese around the edge and the other ingredients are thoroughly mixed in.

6. Gradually add the rest of the cheese and wine, as well as some of the Tequila, stirring them in alternately.

7. Taste and add more Tequila to taste.

8. Once the mixture has completely melted, place the pot on a spirit or gel burner.

9. Season to taste with pepper, in the pot or on the plates. Ay, caramba! Grab your forks!

36 HEART-WARMING FONDUE WITH HOMEMADE RED PESTO

INGREDIENTS

- 1 clove of garlic, peeled and halved
- 400 ml white wine
- 800 g fondue mix
- 6 to 8 teaspoons homemade red pesto (see page 119)
- 500 g white bread

METHOD

1. Rub the fondue pot with the garlic, which you can then leave in the pot or remove, according to taste.

2. Heat 50 ml of the wine in the fondue pot at medium temperature.

3. When the wine is hot, add ¼ of the fondue mix.

4. Stir in a figure of eight or circle, making sure that all the cheese around the edge is mixed in.

5. When the mixture begins to melt, gradually add the rest of the cheese and wine and a little of the pesto.

6. Taste before working in the rest of the pesto and add more if required. What a fragrant aroma!

7. Season to taste with pepper, in the pot or on the plates.

O&CO.
olive oil

RED PESTO

INGREDIENTS

- 135 g dried tomatoes in oil
- 1 to 2 cloves of garlic
- 20 g pine nuts
- 160 ml olive oil
- 20 g dried basil
- Salt and pepper

METHOD

1. Peel the garlic.

2. Put all the ingredients into a mixer. Mix for about 10 seconds.

3. Scrape the edges of the mixer with a spatula to bring the ingredients into the middle.

4. Mix again for 10 seconds. For a smoother paste, repeat.

37 FONDUE WITH HOMEMADE GREEN PESTO

INGREDIENTS

- 1 clove of garlic, peeled and halved
- 400 ml white wine
- 800 g fondue mix
- 6 to 8 teaspoons homemade green pesto (see page 123)
- 500 g white bread

METHOD

1. Rub the fondue pot with the garlic, which you can then leave in the pot or remove, according to taste.

2. Heat a little of the wine in the fondue pot at medium temperature.

3. Add ¼ of the fondue mix.

4. Stir throughout preparation in a zigzag or circle, making sure that all the cheese around the edge is mixed in.

5. When the cheese begins to melt, gradually add the rest alternately with the wine, then stir in some of the pesto.

6. Taste and add more pesto if required.

7. Once the mixture has completely melted, place the fondue pot on a spirit or gel burner.

8. Season to taste with pepper, in the pot or on the plates.

GREEN PESTO

INGREDIENTS

- 20 g fresh basil
- 100 ml extra-virgin olive oil
- 120 g pine nuts
- 80 g parmesan
- 2 cloves of garlic
- Salt and pepper

METHOD

1. Lightly toast the pine nuts in a non-stick pan at medium heat until they are slightly golden (three to six minutes).

2. Remove the stalks from the basil leaves.

3. Coarsely grate the parmesan and crush the garlic.

4. Put the pine nuts, basil leaves, parmesan and garlic into an electric mixer and mix to a coarse consistency.

5. Add half the olive oil and mix again to produce a slightly finer paste. Pour in the rest of the olive oil and mix until you have the preferred consistency.

6. Season to taste with salt and pepper.

A LITTLE TOUR OF THE VEGETABLE GARDEN

38 FONDUE AMONG FRIENDS – WITH GARLIC AND SHALLOTS

INGREDIENTS

- 400 ml white wine
- 800 g fondue mix
- 4 to 6 cloves of garlic and 1 to 2 shallots
- 500 g white bread

METHOD

1. Chop the shallots and the garlic, setting one clove aside.

2. Peel and halve the remaining garlic clove and rub the fondue pot with it.

3. Heat about 50 ml of the wine in the fondue pot at medium temperature.

4. When the wine begins to heat up, add the chopped garlic and shallots and simmer for about a minute.

5. Add ¼ of the fondue mix.

6. Stir in a figure of eight or circle, making sure the cheese around the edge is mixed in.

7. When the mixture starts to melt, gradually add the rest of the wine and cheese, stirring them in alternately.

8. Once the mixture has completely melted, place the fondue pot on a spirit or gel burner.

9. Season to taste with pepper, in the pot or on the plates.

39 FONDUE WITH VEGETABLES

INGREDIENTS

- 1 clove of garlic
- 400 ml white wine
- 800 g fondue mix
- 250 g carrots, zucchini and celery, cooked and diced
- 500 g white bread

NOTE

This is a great way of persuading kids to eat vegetables!

METHOD

1. Rub the fondue pot with the garlic, which you can then leave in the pot or remove, according to taste.

2. Heat about 50 ml of the wine in the fondue pot at medium temperature.

3. When the wine begins to heat up, add the vegetables and simmer for about a minute.

4. Add ¼ of the fondue mix.

5. Stir in a figure of eight or circle, making sure the cheese around the edge is mixed in.

6. When the mixture begins to melt, gradually add the rest of the cheese and wine, stirring them in alternately.

7. Once the mixture has completely melted, place the fondue pot on a spirit or gel burner.

8. Season to taste with pepper, in the pot or on the plates.

40 FONDUE WITH EGGPLANT CAVIAR

INGREDIENTS

- 1 clove of garlic
- 400 ml white wine
- 800 g fondue mix
- 200 g eggplant caviar (see page 133)
- 500 g white bread

METHOD

1. Rub the fondue pot with the garlic, which you can then leave in the pot or remove, according to taste.

2. Heat about 50 ml of the wine in the fondue pot at medium temperature.

3. When the wine is hot, add ¼ of the fondue mix.

4. Stir in a figure of eight or circle, making sure that the cheese around the edge is mixed in.

5. When the mixture begins to melt, gradually add the rest of the wine and cheese, stirring them in alternately. When you have worked in ¾ of the fondue mix, add the eggplant caviar, continuing to stir gently, then the rest of the wine and cheese.

6. Once the mixture has completely melted, place the fondue pot on a spirit or flammable gel burner.

7. Season to taste with pepper, in the pot or on the plates.

EGGPLANT CAVIAR

INGREDIENTS

- 2 eggplants
- Juice of half a lemon
- 50 ml olive oil
- 2 cloves of garlic
- Salt and pepper

METHOD

1. Cut the eggplants into small pieces and cook them in boiling water for 10 minutes.

2. Drain off the water, squeeze the eggplants, and put them into a mixer. Add salt and pepper and a little lemon juice.

3. Crush the garlic and add it.

4. Put the eggplant caviar into a bowl and refrigerate for half an hour.

41 BEWITCHING FONDUE – WITH PUMPKIN

INGREDIENTS

- 1 clove of garlic, peeled and halved
- 300 ml white wine
- 800 g fondue mix
- 250 g pumpkin, cooked, seasoned and puréed
- 500 g white bread

NOTE

Instead of using a pot, you can serve the fondue in a large hollowed-out pumpkin, warmed in the oven.

METHOD

1. Rub the fondue pot with the garlic, which you can then leave in the pot or remove, according to taste.

2. Heat about 50 ml of the wine in the fondue pot at medium temperature.

3. When the wine is hot, add ¼ of the fondue mix and let it melt.

4. Stir throughout preparation in a zigzag or circle, making sure the cheese around the edge is mixed in.

5. Gradually stir in more wine and cheese, and when ¾ of the cheese has melted, add the pumpkin, then the rest of the fondue mix. The amount of wine is a basic guideline for a fondue without additional ingredients, so if the fondue becomes too runny, don't add all of it.

6. Once the mixture has completely melted, place the fondue pot on a spirit or flammable gel burner.

7. Season to taste with pepper, in the pot or on the plates.

42 FONDUE WITH ZUCCHINI

INGREDIENTS

- 1 clove of garlic
- 400 ml white wine
- 800 g fondue mix
- 1 zucchini, finely diced
- 500 g white bread

TIP

If preferred, purée the zucchini and add it at stage 7.

METHOD

1. Rub the fondue pot with the garlic, which you can then leave in the pot or remove, according to taste.

2. Heat about 50 ml of the wine in the fondue pot at medium temperature.

3. When the wine begins to heat up, add the zucchini pieces and simmer for about a minute.

4. Add another 50 ml of the wine and heat.

5. When the wine is hot, add ¼ of the fondue mix and let it melt.

6. Stir in a figure of eight or circle, making sure the cheese around the edge and the zucchini are thoroughly mixed in.

7. When the mixture begins to melt, gradually add the rest of the cheese and wine, stirring them in alternately.

8. Once the mixture has completely melted, place the fondue pot on a spirit or flammable gel burner.

9. Season to taste with pepper, in the pot or on the plates.

43 COUNTRY-STYLE FONDUE WITH LEEK

INGREDIENTS

- 1 clove of garlic
- 400 ml white wine
- 800 g fondue mix
- 250 g leek, finely sliced and cooked
- 500 g white bread

METHOD

1. Rub the fondue pot with the garlic, which you can then leave in the pot or remove, according to taste.

2. Heat about 50 ml of the wine in the fondue pot at medium temperature.

3. When the wine is hot, add ¼ of the fondue mix.

4. Stir throughout preparation in a figure of eight or circle, making sure the cheese around the edge is mixed in.

5. When the mixture begins to melt, gradually add more cheese and wine, stirring them in alternately. Add the leek before working in the rest of the cheese.

6. When the mixture has completely melted, place the fondue pot on a spirit or flammable gel burner.

7. Season to taste with pepper, in the pot or on the plates.

44 PROVENÇAL-STYLE FONDUE WITH HOMEMADE RATATOUILLE

INGREDIENTS

- 1 clove of garlic, peeled and halved
- 300 ml white wine
- 800 g fondue mix
- 250 g ratatouille (see page 143)
- 500 g white bread

METHOD

1. Rub the fondue pot with the garlic, which you can then leave in the pot or remove, according to taste.

2. Heat 50 ml of the wine in the fondue pot at medium temperature.

3. When the wine is hot, add ¼ of the fondue mix and stir in a figure of eight or circle throughout preparation.

4. Gradually add the rest of the wine and cheese, stirring them in alternately. When you have worked in about half the cheese, add the ratatouille and continue cooking.

5. When the mixture has completely melted, place the fondue pot on a spirit or flammable gel burner. Your fondue is ready to enjoy!

6. Season to taste with pepper, in the pot or on the plates.

RATATOUILLE

INGREDIENTS

- 4 tomatoes
- 1 good-sized zucchini
- 1 eggplant
- 2 onions
- 1 red or green bell pepper
- 2 cloves of garlic
- 4 tablespoons olive oil
- 3 sprigs of parsley
- 2 sprigs of thyme
- 100 ml water
- Salt and pepper

METHOD

1. Cut up the parsley, peel the onions and garlic. Remove the seeds, the green heart and white parts of the pepper, the head and tail of the egg-plant, and the stems of the tomatoes. Dice or slice the vegetables finely.

2. Heat two tablespoons of olive oil in a saucepan, add the chopped onions and fry them for a few minutes at medium heat until golden brown, then add the tomatoes, and cook for a few minutes, stirring from time to time.

3. Add all the other vegetables, flavor with garlic, parsley, thyme and two tablespoons of olive oil, season with salt and pepper, add the water, cover and simmer for an hour at low heat, stirring at regular intervals.

45 ITALIAN-STYLE FONDUE WITH OLIVES

INGREDIENTS

- 1 clove of garlic, peeled and halved
- 400 ml white wine
- 800 g fondue mix
- A handful of green olives, pitted
- 500 g white bread

TIP

To vary the taste, use black or chili-stuffed olives.

METHOD

1. Dice the olives.

2. Rub the fondue pot with the garlic, which you can then leave in the pot or remove, according to taste.

3. Heat 50 ml of the wine in the fondue pot at medium temperature.

4. When the wine begins to heat up, add ¼ of the fondue mix.

5. Stir gently in a figure of eight or circle, making sure the cheese around the edge is mixed in.

6. When the cheese begins to melt, gradually add the rest, stirring it in alternately with the wine and the olives.

7. Once the mixture has completely melted, place the fondue pot on a spirit or flammable gel burner.

8. Season to taste with pepper, in the pot or on the plates.

46 SUCCULENT FONDUE WITH DRIED TOMATOES

INGREDIENTS

- 1 clove of garlic, peeled and halved
- 400 ml white wine
- 800 g fondue mix
- 200 g dried tomatoes in oil
- 500 g white bread

METHOD

1. Cut the dried tomatoes into small pieces.

2. Rub the fondue pot with the garlic, which you can then leave in the pot or remove, according to taste.

3. Heat 50 ml of the wine in the fondue pot at medium temperature.

4. When the wine starts to heat up, cook the dried tomatoes for about a minute.

5. Add about another 50 ml of wine and heat.

6. Once the wine is hot, add ¼ of the fondue mix.

7. Stir gently in a figure of eight or circle, making sure the cheese around the edge is mixed in.

8. When the cheese begins to melt, add the rest, stirring it in alternately with the wine.

9. When the mixture has completely melted, place the fondue pot on a spirit or flammable gel burner.

10. Season to taste with pepper, in the pot or on the plates.

47 MELT-IN-THE-MOUTH FONDUE WITH HOMEMADE ONION CHUTNEY

INGREDIENTS

- 1 clove of garlic, peeled and sliced
- 400 ml white wine
- 800 g fondue mix
- 200 g onion chutney (see page 151)
- 500 g white bread

METHOD

1. Rub the fondue pot with the garlic, which you can then leave in the pot or remove, according to taste.

2. Heat about 50 ml of the wine in the fondue pot at medium temperature.

3. When the wine is hot, add ¼ of the fondue mix.

4. Stir in a figure of eight or circle, making sure the cheese around the edge is mixed in.

5. When the cheese begins to melt, add the rest, stirring it in alternately with wine. When you have worked in ¾ of your fondue mixture, add the onion chutney, continuing to stir gently.

6. When the mixture has completely melted, place the fondue pot on a spirit or flammable gel burner.

7. Season to taste with pepper, in the pot or on the plates.

ONION CHUTNEY

INGREDIENTS

- 6 red or medium-strength yellow onions
- 200 ml red wine
- 50 ml balsamic vinegar
- 50 g caster sugar
- 20 g butter
- 1 tablespoon honey
- Salt and pepper

METHOD

1. Peel and finely chop the onions.

2. Melt the butter in a saucepan over low heat, add the onions and season with salt.

3. Cook the onions for three minutes, then add the honey to caramelize them.

4. Add the caster sugar, the red wine and the balsamic vinegar.

5. Bring the mixture to the boil, mixing it from time to time, and cook until the liquid has been almost completely absorbed.

6. Adjust the seasoning with salt and add pepper as required.

48 A FONDUE FOR THE FALL – WITH CHESTNUTS

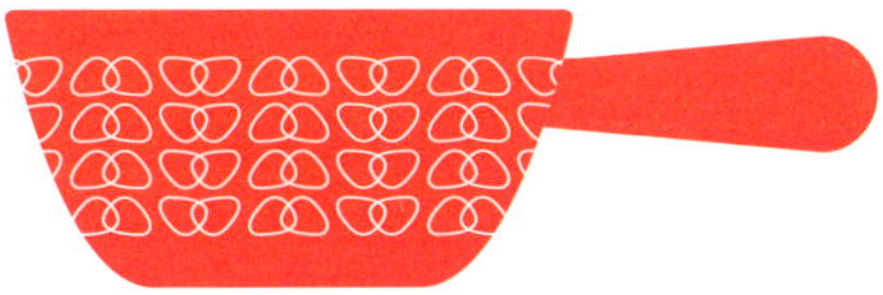

INGREDIENTS

- 1 clove of garlic, peeled and sliced
- 400 ml white wine
- 800 g fondue mix
- 200 g chestnuts, cooked and diced
- 500 g white bread

METHOD

1. Rub the fondue pot with the garlic, which you can then leave in the pot or remove, according to taste.

2. Heat 50 ml of the wine in the fondue pot at medium temperature.

3. When the wine starts to heat up, add the chestnuts and cook for about a minute.

4. Add ¼ of the fondue mix.

5. Stir throughout preparation in a figure of eight or circle, making sure the cheese around the edge is mixed in.

6. When the mixture begins to melt, add the rest of the cheese and wine, stirring them in alternately.

7. When the mixture has completely melted, place the fondue pot on a spirit or flammable gel burner.

8. Season to taste with pepper, in the pot or on the plates.

49 HERBAL FONDUE WITH NETTLES

INGREDIENTS

- 1 clove of garlic, peeled and halved
- 400 ml lager
- A tiny piece of ginger, grated
- 800 g fondue mix
- 2 tablespoons of dried nettles, ground to a powder
- 4 medium-sized potatoes per person as an alternative or a supplement to bread

NOTE

Nettles make this fondue very digestible. It goes wonderfully well with potatoes.

METHOD

1. Rub the fondue pot with the garlic, which you can then leave in the pot or remove, according to taste.

2. Mix the cheese, grated ginger, nettles and lager over a medium heat.

3. Allow to rest for 15 to 20 minutes.

4. Heat the mixture gently at low temperature.

5. Stir in a circle, making sure that none of the ingredients sticks to the pot.

6. If the fondue is too runny, add 2 teaspoons potato or corn flour (US: corn starch). If it is too thick, add a little lager.

7. When the mixture has completely melted, place the fondue pot on a spirit or flammable gel burner.

8. Season to taste with pepper, in the pot or on the plates.

FROM THE FRUIT TREE

50 ENERGIZING FONDUE WITH DRIED APRICOTS

INGREDIENTS

- 1 clove of garlic, peeled and halved
- 400 ml white wine
- 800 g fondue mix
- 200 g dried apricots, finely chopped
- 500 g white bread

METHOD

1. Rub the fondue pot with the garlic, which you can then leave in the pot or remove, according to taste.

2. Heat about 50 ml of the wine in the fondue pot at medium temperature.

3. When the wine is hot, add ¼ of the fondue mix.

4. Stir throughout preparation in a figure of eight or circle, making sure the cheese around the edge is mixed in.

5. Once the mixture begins to melt, add the rest of the cheese and wine, stirring them in alternately. When you have worked in ¾ of your fondue mix, add the dried apricots, and stir gently. You're almost there!

6. When the mixture has completely melted, place the fondue pot on a spirit or flammable gel burner.

7. Season to taste with pepper, in the pot or on the plates.

51 FONDUE WITH APPLE JUICE – CHILDHOOD MEMORIES

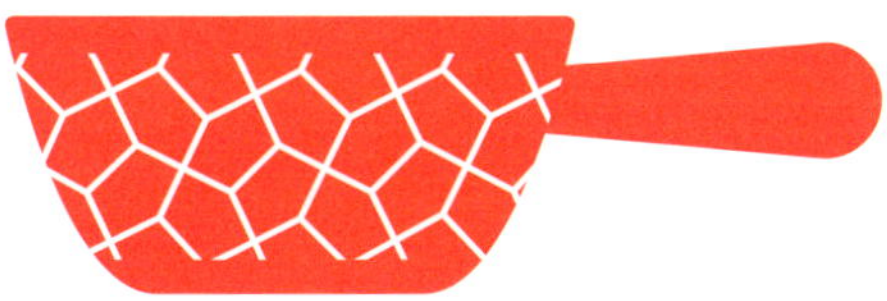

INGREDIENTS

- 1 clove of garlic, peeled and sliced
- 400 ml apple juice (non-carbonated)
- 800 g fondue mix
- 500 g white bread

METHOD

1. Rub the fondue pot with the garlic, which you can then leave in the pot or remove, according to taste.

2. Heat about 50 ml of the apple juice in the fondue pot at medium temperature.

3. When the apple juice is hot, add ¼ of the fondue mix.

4. Stir throughout preparation in a figure of eight or draw apples with your wooden spatula, making sure the cheese around the edge is mixed in.

5. When the cheese begins to melt, gradually add the rest, stirring it in alternately with the apple juice.

6. If the fondue is too thick, add a little apple juice. If it is too runny, add some potato flour.

7. When the mixture has completely melted, place the pot on a spirit or flammable gel burner. You're ready to taste your fondue!

8. Season to taste with pepper, in the pot or on the plates.

52 SMOOTH FONDUE FLAVORED WITH APPLE PURÉE

INGREDIENTS

- 1 clove of garlic, peeled and sliced
- 400 ml white wine
- 800 g fondue mix
- 250 g homemade apple purée (see page 165)
- 500 g white bread

METHOD

1. Rub the fondue pot with the garlic, which you can then leave in the pot or remove, according to taste.

2. Heat 50 ml of the wine in the fondue pot at medium temperature.

3. Once the wine is hot, add ¼ of the fondue mix.

4. Stir throughout preparation in a figure of eight or circle.

5. Add more wine and cheese, stirring them in alternately.

6. Once ¾ of the cheese has melted, add the apple purée, then the rest of the fondue mix.

7. When the mixture has completely melted, place the pot on a spirit or flammable gel burner and taste your fondue.

8. Season to taste with pepper, in the pot or on the plates.

APPLE PURÉE

INGREDIENTS

- 1 kg apples
- 250 ml water

METHOD

1. Peel the apples, cut them roughly into quarters, removing the pips, and put them in a saucepan.

2. Add enough water to reach a level of 1 or 2 centimeters from the bottom of the pan, cover and cook over a low heat for about ten minutes until the apples are soft.

3. Purée with a mixer.

IN AN EMERGENCY: WHERE IN THE WORLD CAN YOU FIND A FONDUE?

1 - S.O.S. Fondue
www.sosfondue.ca, home delivery, Quebec

2 - The Matterhorn Swiss Restaurant
San Francisco, USA

3 - Stable
Washington DC, USA

4 - Urban Fondue
Portland, USA

5 - Swissfondue
La Paz, Bolivia

6 - Fondue en San Javier
Tandil, Argentina

7 - La Fondue
Varadero, Kuba

8 - Fondueboden
Stockholm, Sweden

9 - La Ribaudière
Antananarivo, Madagascar

10 - The Melting Pot
Doha, Qatar

11 - The Food Studio
Vashi Navi Mumbai, Maharashtra, India

12 - Franco-Thai Place Restaurant
Chiang Mai, Thailand

13 - Auberge du Soleil
Kampot, Cambodia

14 - Chesa, The Peninsula Hotel
Hong Kong

15 - Cheese Craft Works
Tokyo, Japan

16 - Fromage [The Cow]
Milton, Australia

WHAT DOES FONDUE MEAN FOR YOU?

Yves Malinjod
Promoter of Swiss cheeses abroad

« Whatever storm is raging, keep calm and eat fondue! »

Barbara Weus
A Breton among the Swiss

Fondue is the soul of the mountain.
Prepared in a few minutes and preferably eaten outdoors. Welcome to comfort and good cheer.

Dorian Rollin
Photographer

« Fondue is simplicity and good humor. »

René Schudel
Chef and fondue lover

The memory of my first fondue: steamed-up windows, **smiling faces and pink cheeks.**

Patrick Rosset
Founder of Le Monde des Épices

Fondue is my whole youth,
and please note, I can't eat it without my family or my friends!

Felix Kindelán
Graphic designer from Berlin

« Whenever I eat fondue, I feel like jumping into the pot. »

Laurent Vieux
Cheesemaker in Muraz, Canton Valais

A customer quoted this maxim to me and I have adopted it:
"Give me health for a long time,
love from time to time,
and work not too often —
but a good fondue all the time!"

ACKNOWLEDGEMENTS

We wish to express our gratitude to the many people who, from near or far, added their "grist to the mill." A BIG thank you therefore to:

The dream team from our publisher, Helvetiq, who immediately believed in the project, and to Valentin Crettaz for pushing the idea forward.

The members of our association, *Les Compagnons du Caquelon*, for their support and advice in matters of cheese.

Steve and Brigida Langel of the Café du Midi in Martigny for enabling us to launch in 2012 what has since then been known worldwide as the "Festival of Fondues" and for the whole crazy adventure.

Léonard Granges from Marchon SA, a specialist in non-food products in Switzerland, who graciously lent us a showroom and provided us with Heidi Cheese Line products.

Alfredo Ralda from Heidi Line for his help with the photo shoots.

Photographer Dorian Rollin and culinary stylist Morgane Cintas for a week of photo shoots full of fun and puns.

Anne Hubert of www.lacerisesurlegateau.fr for the loan of her wonderful table linen.

Isabelle Wüthrich of Les Fils Maye and the Vieux family of Vieux Fromages for providing us with raw materials. The quality of the local products is apparent in every mouthful!

Herbalist Marlène Galleti for the tasty nettle recipe that she allowed us to use in this book.

Camille Bossetti and Thomas Roulin for providing us with their favorite recipe for vegan fondue.

Translator Alison Metzger-Martin for her help in presenting fondue in the language of Shakespeare.

Davina Carrel from Amstein SA for her excellent beer brewing advice.

Njomza Selmani from the Association *Pain Suisse*, who drew our attention to a variety of bread recipes. Who else would have thought of eating a fondue with a brioche-style plaited loaf?

Manuela Sonderegger of Switzerland Cheese Marketing AG for her help and sound advice on various technical matters.

Yan Sutterlin, Co-Director of La Fromathèque in Martigny, who specializes in sheep's and goat's cheese.

Our faithful testers, who devoted themselves body and soul to numerous tasting sessions.

Our families and friends, naturally, who had ringside seats in this adventure for more than one and a half years.

And you, enquiring epicureans, who hold this noble work in your hands.

Photo shoots supported by HEIDI CHEESE LINE, VIEUX FROMAGE and LES FILS MAYE

HEIDI®
CHEESE LINE

Swiss Fondue
The Fine Art of Fondue in 52 Tasty Recipes
ISBN: 978-3-03964-076-8

Cover design & illustrations: Florian Bellon
Interior design: Florian Bellon
Additional layout support: Elżbieta Kownacka
Photos: Dorian Rollin
Additional photos: Pixabay (pages 10, 22, 28, 166), Helvetiq (pages 40, 76, 90, 118, 120, 130, 142, 148)
Translation from French: Alison Metzger-Martin
Proofreading: Karin Waldhauser
Printed in the Czech Republic

HEL·· VETiQ helvetiq.com

MIX
Paper from responsible sources
FSC www.fsc.org FSC® C014138